When The Caterpillar Met The Butterfly

A Love Letter To Growth, Change, and Becoming

Kailey Volpetti, MA, LMHC

BookLeaf Publishing

India | USA | UK

Made with ❤ on the BookLeaf Publishing Platform

www.bookleafpub.in

www.bookleafpub.com

Dedication

For those on the journey,

growing, changing, evolving—

May you embrace every stage of your
becoming.

Acknowledgement

This collection would not exist without the love and support of so many. To those who have walked alongside me in this journey—your belief in me has meant more than words can express. To the moments, lessons, and quiet transformations that shaped these poems—thank you for teaching me to see the beauty in change. And to you, dear reader—thank you for allowing my words to be a part of your journey.

Preface

Poetry has always been my way of making sense of the world—of capturing fleeting emotions, quiet transformations, and the beauty of change. As a child therapist, I have witnessed the beauty of transformation—the way growth can be slow yet profound, the way resilience takes shape in the smallest moments. This collection is inspired by this very same journey, by the courage it takes to step into the unknown, to trust the process of becoming. Like a caterpillar transforming into a butterfly, we all move through stages of change, learning to embrace the in-between. This collection of poems is for those still unfolding, and also for those who have already found their wings.

To honor confidentiality, client names and identifying details have been changed. This collection reflects a blend of collective experiences rather than having any specific individual subjectivity attached to it. All are shared with deep care and respect.

When the caterpillar asked the butterfly, "Will I be okay?"

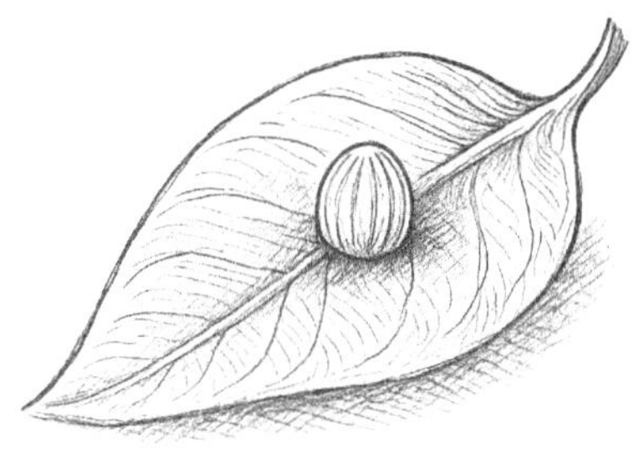

Unknowing of the beauty
that awaits,
And all of the pain it takes
to get there,
The caterpillar looks up—
wide-eyed, uncertain.

The butterfly,
in all of her beauty and knowing,
smiles and replies,
"Yes."

A single word,
A quiet truth,
With the knowing that
to become beautiful
is to let go,
To shed everything you were,
And begin anew.

Who...are you?

She looked up at the blue caterpillar
with eyes wide and heart pounding.

Who am I?

"I am the sky,
Endless.
With cloudy eyes that
pour like hurricanes.
I am the whisper of wind,
that you fear will vanish
as soon as it arrives.

I am the peeks of sunlight through your
curtains
on a lazy summer day,
rarer than rainbows
and just as fleeting."

"I know who I am," she whispered.
"And you–
You too are becoming something beautiful."

I heard there's money to be made in selling rare butterflies

There was a man named Yoshi
who could catch butterflies
better than anyone—
Thousands of dollars
on almost extinct species,
Wings spread,
spanning eleven inches wide.
A marvel!
Breathtaking in all sense of the word.

He would pin their wings down,
transporting them across oceans
To men with too much money,

too much time,
and not enough sense
to know—

A butterfly is most rare,
most beautiful,
when she is free...

Growth

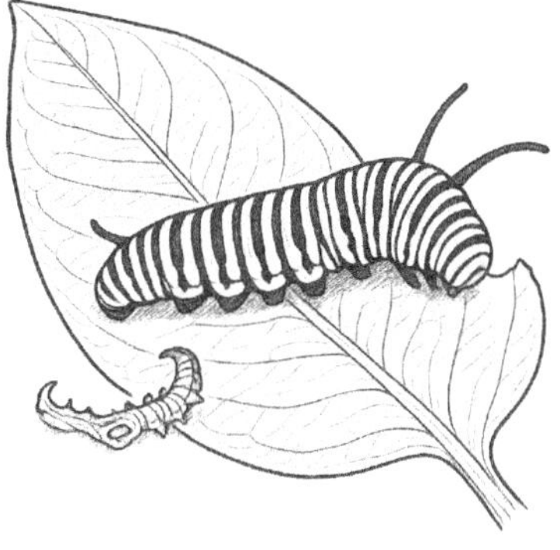

The butterfly catches her reflection
in the window.

And if she looks closely,
she sees the caterpillar—
and smiles.

Paper Boats

Today, I follow YouTube tutorials on how to
make origami boats—
"easy"
"beginner"
"for kids"—
while sitting in my office with two windows
and an air conditioner with a remote.
Success feels like a cool breeze and an open
window.

I am teleported back—
plastic couches,
a window that barely cracked open,
sweat dripping down the small of my back.

Climbing over piles of snow,
unbuttoning coats the second we walked
inside,
nothing felt more like summer
than my Nonno's apartment
in the dead of winter in Brooklyn.

"It's that boiler room!!" we'd cry, peeling off
layers.
(I think I just realized why my Nonno always
sat by the door.)

My Nonno stood five foot nothing
and spoke just about nothing in English.
A full head of gray hair,
a laugh that rumbled through the walls.
He told stories we didn't understand,
but he told them with joy.

"He's crazy!" my mother would scream.

Sometimes, I'd sit with him as he doodled—
silly faces, big ears, wide smiles
lining the kitchen walls like tiny ghosts of
laughter.

He made paper boats with shaky hands,
and I loved them.

I never knew how,
but I'd try to recreate them,
folding corners, creasing edges,
Always close—
Never quite the same.

Big ones. Small ones.
Even smaller ones.
I was always fascinated.

I wish I had asked him to teach me,
I wish I knew who taught him,
I wish I could teach him how to make paper
stars...
It wasn't magic, but it was mine.

Now, I sit in a cold room with fully opened
windows,
grateful.

I wonder how the boat ride to America felt.
The weight of the ocean between him

and The American Dream.

I wish I knew him.
But all I have are paper boats—
and they aren't even his.

I figured out how to make them on my own.

On my own.
On my own.

But maybe that's what he wanted.

To show me that my hands can still create,
even when they shake.
That we build our lives in small folds—
corner by corner, crease by crease—
until we shape something that carries
us forward.

Maybe he didn't need to teach me.
Maybe, just by being here, I already learned.

Maybe, I was always meant to make it
On my own.

The Butterfly Effect

I rarely drink tea,
but on this gray, rain-washed morning,
I slipped a few bags into my purse
before heading to work.

A small child's loved one had died—
their first brush with loss,
their first taste of what it means
to be human.
Suffering, woven into our bones,
An inevitability
they do not yet understand.

What do you say to a child
with tears in their eyes
and the question, "*Why?*"

I take a breath.

"Tell me about them."

And so the stories spill—
memories bubbling up,
soft smiles through sniffles,
until—

"They used to make me tea"

I reach into my bag.
There it is.
Their eyes widen, shining—
"It's the exact same one!"

And suddenly,
we are no longer cross-legged
on the carpet of my small office.
We are running into the kitchen,
boiling water,
dunking tea bags,
watching steam rise
as laughter stirs the air.

I think this is how
God winks at us.

Quiet Proof

No peace is greater
than quiet moments—
a warm couch,
an open window,
counting planes as they pass
through the amber glow of sunset,
a breeze, light as a whisper.

In this stillness,
I feel the weight lift—
proof that even the hardest days
fade into something softer,
brighter,
if you just keep going.

DUMBO, Brooklyn, NYC

Hand in hand,
smiles and adventure,
soft breeze, waves,
pizza and ice cream—
an easy love.

I close my eyes
and teleport back
to salty tears,
drowsy red eyes,
what felt like the end—
and quite possibly
could have been.

Until the most important decision of my life:

"I need to go to the hospital."

How wonderful it is
to be loved,
to be known so fully,
to have held on
until they found me—
like a head-on collision,
splitting my life
into before
and after.

Ever since.

El Guardián de las Monarcas

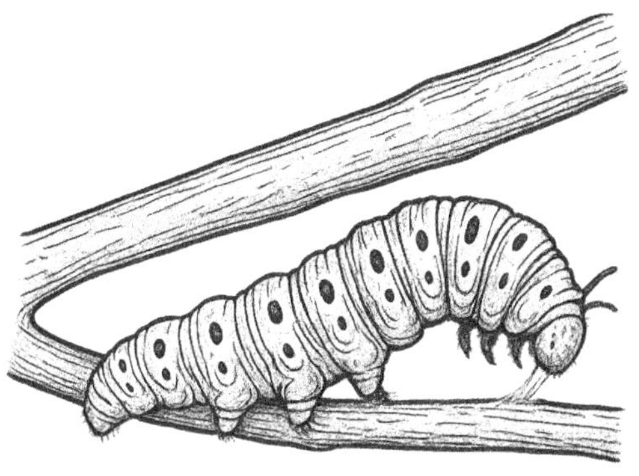

Before the snow begins to fall,
and a sharp chill settles in the air,
millions of monarch butterflies
somehow know—
it is time to take flight.

They embark on their journey,
two thousand miles south,
leaving Canada behind,
traveling all the way
to Michoacán, México.

There, a man named
Homero Gómez González—
gentler than a butterfly
landing softly on your shoulder—
called them Lovers of the Sun
and Souls of the Dead.

With open arms,
He welcomed the world
to witness the miracle:
thousands upon thousands
of bright orange wings,
edged in black,
spotted in white,
returning home.

To share such beauty,
to protect it,
must require a love
so deep,
so profoundly pure,
so human.

But what is more human
than love—

the instinct to Nurture,
to Protect,
to Preserve?

And what is more human
than greed—
the hunger to Own,
to Take,
to Consume?

Than hands that plant trees
and hands that burn forests?
Minds that dream of sanctuary
and minds that dream of profit?
A heart that weeps for wonder,
a heart that kills for power?

In January 2020,
Homero Gómez González—
The Guardian of the Monarchs—
Vanished.
Two weeks later,
they found him.
At the bottom of a well.

The human body
is capable of both
gentleness and violence,
capable of saving life
and taking it away.
We carry within us
great light—
a fire that warms,
a fire that guides,
And great darkness—
a fire that consumes,
a fire that destroys.

And so, the butterflies return,
undeterred by the weight of the world.

Some say he, too,
joins the migration now,
returning each year
to the sanctuary,
with no agenda,
no revenge—
only beauty,
offered freely,
a gift we are privileged

to witness,
again and again.

They remind us,
year after year,
that even in loss,
there is return.
Even in sorrow,
there is renewal.
Because nothing truly vanishes—
not the Spirit,
not the Fight,
not the Light that once burned
in a man who dared to protect
what others sought to destroy.

Still, they fly.
And still, we watch,
learning,
remembering,
Becoming.

A Recipe for Re-invention

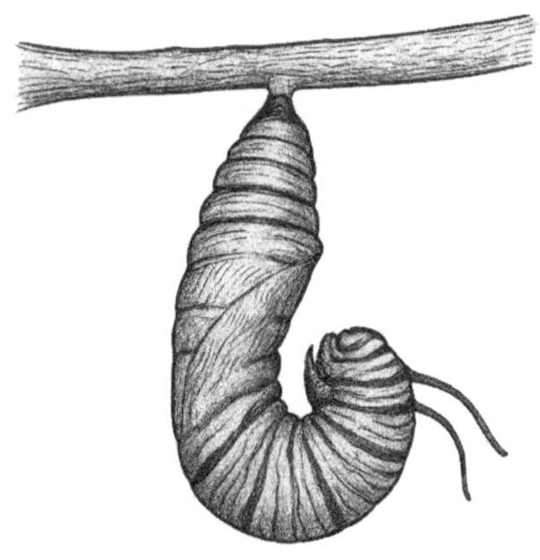

Ingredients:

•1 strong foundation of self-confidence and core values

•2 cups of resilience

•1 heaping scoop of bravery

•A dash of unconditional love (or more, to taste)

•1 life-altering event (handle with caution)

•Patience, as much as you can gather

•1 or more healthy connections

•A sprinkle of vulnerability

•A variety of therapeutic approaches (experiment as needed)

•Time (unknown quantity)

•Optional: a pinch of humor to lighten the process

Note: Some steps may need to be repeated several times.

Instructions:

Step 1:
Preheat your core values and self-confidence until warm but flexible.

Step 2:
In a large mixing bowl, combine resilience, bravery, and unconditional love. Stir gently but consistently—this mixture will hold everything together later.

Step 3:

Carefully introduce a life-changing event. WARNING: This ingredient is unpredictable and may cause instability. Side effects may include:

       •Deep sorrow or grief
       •High anxiety
       •Identity confusion
       •Loss of direction
       •Addiction or destructive behaviors
       •In extreme cases: emotional or existential crisis

Step 4:
Let sit. The waiting period is indeterminate—some transformations occur overnight, while others take years to fully develop.

Step 5:
Once the mixture settles, slowly fold in patience, vulnerability, and at least one healthy connection. Add more as desired—there is no limit to how much support you can use.

Step 6:
Periodically check for stability. If the mixture starts to separate, reintroduce patience and support as needed.

Step 7:
When ready, apply therapy. Note: Not all therapy types will work the same way. If ineffective, try another method or seek a new practitioner.

Step 8:
Allow the mixture to cool. During this time, carefully remove any toxicity. This may include:

- Negative influences (people or environments)
- Destructive habits (substances, self-sabotage)
- Unhealthy comparisons (social media, unrealistic expectations)

Step 9:

If all previous steps were followed with care, you may begin to see signs of rapid growth. These may include:

  - •A renewed sense of identity
  - •Radical self-acceptance
  - •Confidence in your evolving self
  - •A positive vision for the future

Step 10:

Enjoy! Transformation is never a one-time recipe—feel free to tweak, refine, and revisit if needed.

Enough

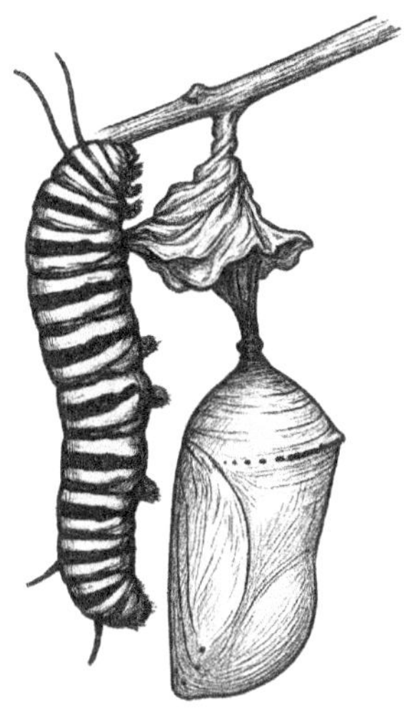

Strength and compassion,
Wide hips and curves,
Gray hair and stretch marks,
I am woman.

No mistakes, no doubt.
There is quiet confidence in my walk—
the kind that does not ask permission,
that takes up space,
that holds its ground, unshaken.

I was thirteen years old
the first time a man
mistook me for a woman.

Walking slightly behind
Mom and Dad,
I wore a floral skirt above my knees,
a black tank top.
It was summertime in Brooklyn.

A car passed—
beeps, lewd remarks.

My mother screamed back:
"She's only thirteen!"

And in that moment,
Horrified, I somehow felt
as if I had done something wrong.

Yet beneath the shock,
with all the insecurities
a teenage girl could carry,
I felt something else.

Confirmation.
That I was beautiful.

From then on,
my mother would tug my shirts higher,
shielding me from a world
I never asked to be seen by.

I'd complain
Not understanding
that my confidence
was never mine—
it was borrowed.

An empty bucket
with a hole in the bottom,
drip,
drip,
dripping away
before I could ever hold it.

Flash forward—twenty years old,
I am the same.

Starving myself to be small,
to be fragile,
to take up less space.

My body shrinking,
my self-worth
down the drain.

The first time I gained weight,
new red stretch marks
etched themselves onto my legs.

My mother noticed immediately.

From my thighs to my calves,
she saw them all.
Her voice made them shameful,
made me feel disgusting.

Comments about my body,
Comparisons to things that were not human.

So, I went on a diet
And she was so proud of me.

To break away from this—
to rebirth the woman I am now—
I had to shed everything
I was taught.

The rules,
The expectations,
The assumptions about myself
and others.

To love myself—
truly love myself—
meant accepting myself,
in every form,
every shape,
every way my body chooses to exist.

This body,
This beautiful body of a woman—
with stretch marks and gray hair,
that lets me walk,
run,
dance,
laugh,
live.

And it turns out,
when you choose what makes *you* happy—
not anyone else,
not their judgments,
not their approval—

you find quiet.

No more voices whispering,
no more thoughts running in circles:
Am I enough?

Because I am.

I am enough for me.

And when I go to sleep,
I am excited for the next day.

No more hatred.
No more suffering.
Just living.

To Those Who Stepped In

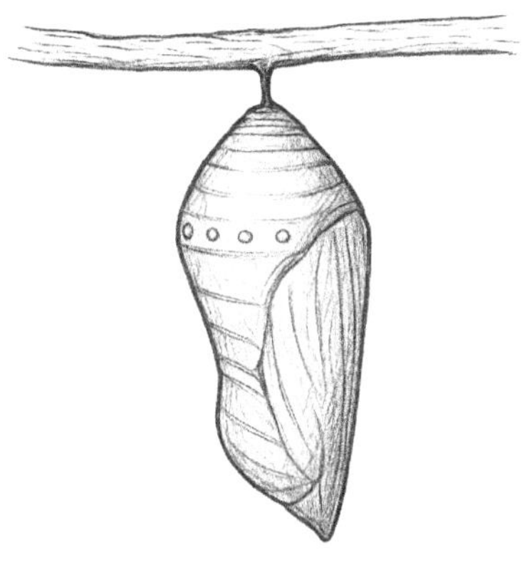

Stepping into the role of
Mother
when no one else
would step up to the plate.

Because pure hearts
protect the forgotten.
Not a replacement—
but because
you were needed.

This is a love letter
to the older sisters,
the aunts, the cousins,
the grandmothers,
the family friends—
who became parents
because it was the right thing to do,
the natural choice.

And somehow,
you became
all the love and support
this human being needed.

A position rarely recognized,
but I see you.
I am you.

Being a therapist to these children,
I can rarely make promises—
but I promise this:

Your love,
your quiet sacrifices,
your unwavering presence—

it means more than you will ever know.

I see your quiet anger,
the lingering confusion—
not towards the child,
but toward those who left them behind.

Yet you do not waver.
You love them anyway.
You show up,
again and again,
as they struggle,
as they hurt,
as they try to make sense
of why the ones who gave them life
were not the ones
who chose to stay.

You never planned for this.
You never asked for it.
But still—
you stayed.

And though this role was never meant to be
yours,

you built something new,
something whole,
something beautiful
out of what was broken.

You turned absence into belonging,
emptiness into home.

And without you,
they may have never known
what love without conditions truly is.

That is everything.

A Pretty Girl Will Never Know

A pretty girl
will never know she is pretty
when she is fed, daily,
a bitter mixture of:
over-concern with others' perceptions,
negativity,
obsession with flaws,
and constant comparison.

How could she not wilt
when she is told,
again and again,
that she is never enough?

What she loves—

not enough.
Who she loves—
not enough.
What she wears,
what she eats,
how she speaks,
how she moves—
never enough.

And it never will be.

If there is one constant in this world,
it is judgment.
People will always watch,
always whisper,
always have their say.

But they do not feel the quiet joy
of your own small victories.
They do not hear the thoughts
that echo in your mind,
the place you must live every day.

And if you are forever at war
with the voice inside you,

peace will never come.

I know this well.
I know the endless ache,
the doubt,
the reaching for worth in the words of others.

But I am not a machine.
I am flesh and bone.
I cannot wind up a smile
or bend myself into the perfect shape
for anyone's approval.

I have stretch marks,
I have scars—
not flaws, but proof.
Proof that I have grown,
that I have healed,
that I have lived.

And what a gift it is—
to take up space,
to breathe,
to exist,
to still be here.

What Was Never Done for Me

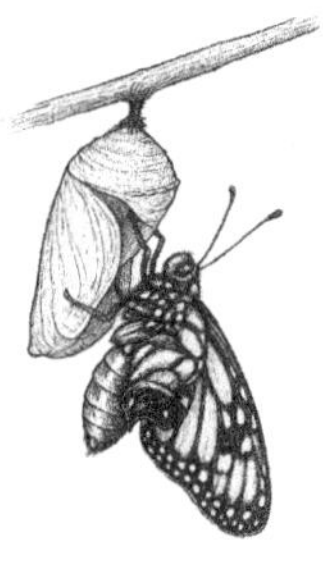

Instead of solving their
marital problems,
my parents sent **me** to therapy.

My therapist worked out of a small,
old house,
converted into an office.

Her waiting room—
once the side entrance to her home—
had old couches, mismatched chairs,
fake plants,
and a fake cat
that looked like it was asleep.

During our sessions,
she led me into the kitchen
and made me hot chocolate.

I don't remember much about her.
Only that she was old,
and once, she asked me:
"Do you believe in God?"

I did.

"You can pray to Him when you are sad."

I did.

A child's prayer:
"Please, God—
Make them stop fighting."

Always unanswered.

I wasn't convinced
that it was God I needed.

Twenty years later—
I, too, become a therapist.

I sit with children,
have hard conversations
with parents,
because if it wasn't done for me,
I will do it for them.

As a child, you don't have much power.
You only have hope.

Hope that someone will listen,
that someone will see you,
that someone will step in.

If the adults in their life fail them,
I hope they find me.

I will not be God.
I will not be their parent.
But I will be there.

And sometimes,
that is enough.

The Other Side of the Tunnel

"It gets better."
"Just keep going."
"There's a light on the other side of the tunnel."

Enter teenage me:
From the *far end* of that tunnel:
"That's gotta be bullshit."

Because people who say that—
they haven't been here.
They don't know what it feels like
to wake up already exhausted,
to drag yourself through another day
that feels exactly like the last.

They must have different brains,
Or easier lives,
Or something I don't.

Maybe they were lucky,
Maybe they were loved differently,
Maybe they just don't understand
what it's like when waiting feels
like **drowning**.

Because how can things ever change?
How does time heal anything
when it only stretches the pain longer?

And then—
it does.

But not all at once.

It starts so small,
you don't even notice.
The one time you said no,
The one time you got up anyway,
The first real laugh in months.

And slowly, painfully,
brick by brick,
you build something new.

They told me it was sink or swim
So I built a fucking boat.

I found the shore,
I built my world,
my way,
from the ground up.

Not because the tunnel suddenly disappeared,
Not because someone pulled me out,

But because I **kept moving**.

Even when I didn't believe in the light,
Even when it felt impossible.

Because somehow,
I decided to try.
Just once.
Then again.

And again.

Until one day,
Without realizing it—
I was already in the sun.

After the Fire

After the fire burns,
forsaking everything in its path,
there is next to nothing left
of what once stood.

It is devastating
to wake up in a world
you no longer recognize—
sifting through soot and ash,
trying to grasp pieces
of what was once there,
only to have them crumble
between your fingertips.

At first, it feels like ruin,
Like loss with no return,
Like nothing good
could ever grow here again.

A few years ago,
I heard a story about trees—
certain species,
with pinecones so thick,
so tightly sealed,
that they can only open
when exposed to fire.

And beneath the charred ground,
wildflowers, roots,
buried deep beneath the earth,
lie dormant for years—
waiting, silently,
for the flames to pass,
so they can finally bloom.

Maybe destruction
is just the beginning.
Maybe the fire

doesn't erase everything—
But reveals what was waiting
to rise from underneath.

What was buried
now reaches for the light.
What was lost
makes way for something new.

And in the place
where ruin once stood,
life begins again.

Bracelets & Black Eyeliner

Moving to the other side
of the country
at fourteen years old
was probably the
stupidest decision
I had no part in.

But as children do—
I had to adjust.

In art class,
I walked right over
and sat next to
a fragile girl with jet-black hair,
thick winged eyeliner,
and handmade beaded bracelets
stacked up to her elbows.

She looked nothing like
the blonde, blue-eyed
popular girls I never
got along with anyway.

We became best friends.

Then one day,
she stopped coming to school.

Days turned into a week.
Weeks into a month.
And just like that,
she was gone,
and I was alone again.

Just when I thought

she had disappeared forever,
she came back—
like a ghost of herself.

But now,
she never went to lunch.

Instead, I followed her
to the nurse's office,
where they watched her eat.

I watched my friend
struggle to swallow
school pizza and carrot sticks,
tears spilling between bites,
while the nurse reminded her—
"You have to eat it."

She begged to go to the bathroom.
And I knew why.

She wanted to reach the back of her throat,
as if it could absolve her
of the sin of hunger.

"*It hurts*," she said,
knees pulled to her chest,
face buried in her hands.

There was nothing I could do
but sit beside her.

And then—
the second dumbest decision
I had no part in —

Moving back
to the other side of the country,
just a year after I had left it.

Only this time,
I was the one who disappeared.

Our friendship was not perfect.
We fought. We argued.
But I wish I could tell her now—

That I never meant to leave,
That I think of her, still,
That in the quiet corners of my memory,

she remains.

Two girls,
sitting side by side,
bearing witness to each other's pain,
in a time and place
where no one else could.

I hope she is happy.
I hope she is safe.
I hope she knows
in that very moment of time,
she was not alone.

The Gifts We Overlook

The bird longs
to swim,
the fish dreams
to fly.

The human
wants wings
to soar,
and gills
to dive—

forgetting he's built sails for the sea,
engines for the sky,
and still he longs
for greener grass,
that's the same
on the other side.

Player 2

There's only one person
I've known since the day they were born.

Only three years younger,
he loved trains,
the color blue,
and peeking at Christmas gifts
before we were allowed to open them.

In the winters,
when the snow piled up
almost as tall as we were,
we built snowmen,

snow forts,
half-made igloos—
our hands numb,
our laughter rising into the cold air.
We didn't go inside
until the sky burned orange with sunset.

In the summers,
we'd get lost for hours,
riding our bikes—
him following me the entire way,
trusting that somehow,
I'd always get us home.

I never considered that
when I left home,
I wasn't just leaving my parents.
I was leaving him too.

An obvious thing,
but somehow,
it hurt even deeper
than I ever imagined.

We witnessed each other
through every phase of life—
from pre-K to high school
to adulthood.

Every struggle.
Every heartbreak.
Every fight.

We were the ones
who saw the aftermath
of the worst days
and the best days
of each other's lives.

To be understood like that—
not through words,
but through shared memories,
through the things that don't need to be
explained.

It's one thing
to hear what someone has been through.
It's another to have lived it with them.
To carry the same moments,

the same memories,
woven into the fabric of who you are.

No matter how far we go,
or how much time passes,
there will always be a piece of me
that belongs to those years—
to the bike rides,
to the snow forts,
to the childhood
we built together.

Not just my best friend,
Not just my player 2,
But the person who knew me before I knew
myself.

To the One Who Wished Me Suffering

Did the words taste like poison
as they left your tongue,
or did they feel like relief?

Did it make the weight lighter,
to pass your pain to me,
to send it somewhere—
anywhere—
just so you wouldn't have to hold it?

I only ever wanted love.
You only ever wanted control.

You spoke of independence,
but only if it kept me bound to you.

You called me broken,
convinced there had to be something,
someone,
some force to blame
for the way I turned out

As if I could only be who I am
by accident.

But I was never yours to mold.

I am not a mistake.
I am not a machine
meant to function
for your comfort.
I am not a reflection
of what you wanted me to be.

I am something else entirely.

I stand up for what I believe in,
I protect my peace,
I have boundaries,
I love deeply and fully.

I am soft,
and strong.
Kind,
and unshakable.
Gentle,
but fierce.

And the best part?

I wake up unafraid,
I move through the world freely,
I laugh without hesitation,
I love without fear.

You wanted me to suffer
But I am still here,
building a life out of everything
you swore I'd never have.

And I wouldn't change a thing.

Always Her

When all you have
is the dream of a better self,
with no promise
that you will ever get there.

You—
the one stuck in the present,
watching the slow
tick, tick, tick
of the clock.

Waiting.
Hoping.

For the future version,
the stronger version,
the one who figured it out,
the one who survived.

But she does not yet exist.
No promises,
No roadmaps,
No guides,

Only the ache
of watching grains of sand
slip, one by one,
down the hourglass.

And somehow,
you have faith—
not in certainty,
but in possibility.

You wish on stars,
pour your soul,
your tears,
your frustration into them,
believing in them

more than you believe in yourself.

But the truth is—
it was never the star,
never the dream,
never some distant version of you
that made it possible.

It was always You.

The one who kept moving,
The one who held on,
The one who survived.

The pieces didn't fall into place—
you put them there.

And when you finally
step into the life
you once only dreamed of,

you will see—

You were always Her.